THE NINJAGO MOVIE

P9-BBP-606

THE ESSENTIAL GUIDE

WRITTEN BY JULIA MARCH

CONTENTS

AN INTRODUCTION
By Master Wu

Imagine a city. A beautiful city, where citizens begin every day by singing. Ninjago City!

Now imagine that city attacked by a nasty villain, again and again. Imagine a battle between father and son, between good and evil.

Only the lessons of a wise ninja master can bring peace to this troubled place. But will my pupils—the Secret Ninja Force—learn those lessons in time?

Step into Ninjago City to find out. Oh, and if you see the villain and his fearsome army, remember to run!

AN INTRODUCTION
By Lord Garmadon

Imagine a city. A beautiful city, where citizens begin every day by screaming. Ninjago City!

Now imagine that city waiting to be conquered by a super-awesome, all-powerful leader, again and again. Imagine a battle between two, unrelated individuals, between a warlord and a ninja.

Only the lessons of an old flute player can spoil this excellent plan. Hopefully his pupils—the Secret Ninja Force—won't be smart enough to learn those lessons in time.

Join the fearsome Shark Army and invade Ninjago City to find out. Get a move on!

NINJAGO CITY

Ninjago City is bustling, vibrant, and prosperous, yet there's something unusual about it, too. There's always lots of construction going on, but the city never grows beyond its limits. It's like the citizens are just rebuilding the same structures over and over again.

Pufferfish blimp is home to a floating sushi restaurant.

Top visitor attractions

The beach
It is very safe to swim here. No sharks have been spotted—yet.

Restaurants
Cuisines from all over the world can be enjoyed here.

Skyscrapers
For the best view, head for the highest floor of the tallest tower. The tallest one this week, that is!

Golden sands and softly lapping waters.

Watery world
Down at the lowest levels of the city, boats bob in the docks or glide along waterways. This is the oldest part of Ninjago City, where many traditional ways of life and older buildings can be found.

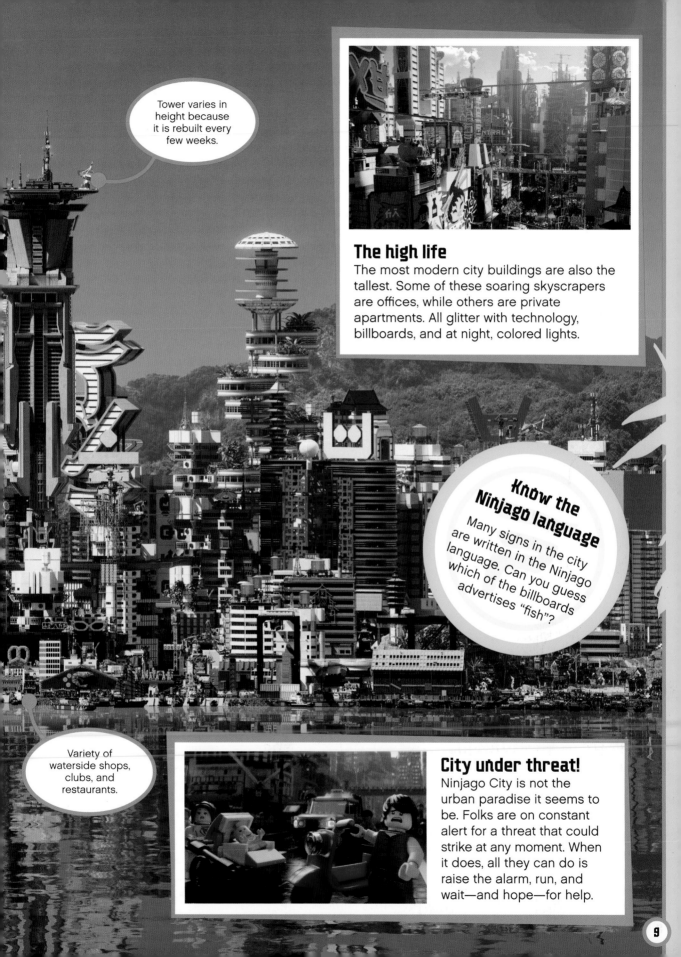

Tower varies in height because it is rebuilt every few weeks.

The high life

The most modern city buildings are also the tallest. Some of these soaring skyscrapers are offices, while others are private apartments. All glitter with technology, billboards, and at night, colored lights.

Know the Ninjago language

Many signs in the city are written in the Ninjago language. Can you guess which of the billboards advertises "fish"?

Variety of waterside shops, clubs, and restaurants.

City under threat!

Ninjago City is not the urban paradise it seems to be. Folks are on constant alert for a threat that could strike at any moment. When it does, all they can do is raise the alarm, run, and wait—and hope—for help.

LORD GARMADON

If he can't rule the city, he'll destroy it

This cruel conqueror is feared by all in Ninjago City. It's because he keeps returning to destroy the place... over and over again. Citizens call Lord Garmadon "The Worst Guy Ever," but only when he is safely out of earshot.

I love conquering!

Did you know?

Lord Garmadon has had many elaborate plots to take over the city in the past. He has led troops of Insect Warriors, Bird Soldiers, and even a Fruit Army.

Best dressed worst guy

Lord Garmadon has four arms, red eyes, and a smile that could sour milk. He also has a relentless drive to crush the Ninjago people (and to crush their city). A guy this bad must dress to oppress, in dark robes and a towering horned helmet.

His helmet makes Lord Garmadon look taller than he is.

Nerds look a little nervous around their bad-tempered boss.

Garmadon's nerds

Garmadon has surrounded himself with a team of IT nerds who labor in his lab night and day. They create the scientific gadgets, weapons, and mechs Garmadon hopes will give him the edge in his next battle with the ninja.

Shark staff is tipped with a blade bearing toothlike spikes.

Garmadon's life goals

Rule Ninjago City
When he finally has control, he might stop smashing up the city. Might.

Defeat the Secret Ninja Force
So far, they've been very, very lucky.

Bond with Lloyd, his long-lost son
Lloyd will have to turn evil first. Then— Garmadons united!

Garmadon likes clothes in dark colors. They go with his mood.

Don't talk back!

Few of Lord Garmadon's soldiers dare to disobey his orders. Complete obedience is expected—and complete silence too, so that Garmadon can enjoy the sound of his own voice shouting commands.

SHARK ARMY

Lord Garmadon is back in Ninjago City with a fishy new fighting force—his Shark Army! With sea creature armor and vehicles to match, they bring chaos to the city. Chaos, but not necessarily victory, much to Garmadon's disgust.

Brown Beanie guy
Strength: Easily blends in with ordinary citizens.
Weakness: No armor makes him vulnerable to attack.

Octopus
Strength: Able to wield several weapons at once.
Weakness: Sometimes gets tangled in his own tentacles.

Hammerhead shark
Strength: Wide angle vision device in helmet.
Weakness: Bulbous eyes are weak spots.

Jellyfish
Strength: Clear-headed, with 360 degree range of vision.
Weakness: Bad team player, lives in his own little bubble.

Pufferfish
Strength: Huge helmet to intimidate enemies.
Weakness: Easily deflated when foes don't back down.

Great white shark
Strengths: Swift, ruthless, and super, super aggressive.
Weakness: Rushes in before orders given, ruining attacks.

Manta Ray Bomber
This flyer swoops low to release its bombs. If it crashes in the sea, the pilot escapes in the cockpit boat.

Lobster
Strengths: A shifty sidestep and powerful pinches.
Weakness: Crabby; wastes time squabbling with allies.

Mobile Crab
The crab vehicle pilot controls a huge pincer with one hand and a shooter with the other. He aims to leave the ninja shell-shocked.

Anglerfish
Strength: Won't let a foe off the hook once caught.
Weakness: Fixating on one foe allows others to escape.

Flying Jelly Sub
Twisting tentacles dangle from this sub when it is airborne. After landing, it scuttles and spins on its rotating legs.

SECRET NINJA FORCE

Every time Lord Garmadon attacks Ninjago City, a mysterious band of ninja appears. The ninja fight him off with their amazing skills, weapons, and mechs. The citizens don't know where these six city saviors come from. They don't really care. They are just glad they come!

White Ninja
Witnesses have said there's something slightly odd—even a little robotic—about the ninja in the ice-white costume.

Silver Ninja
This ninja goes with the flow. One moment she's as silent as a shadow, the next she's a spinning, spear-wielding warrior.

Green Ninja
The ninja in the green robes seems to be the leader—the others often gather around him. Folks who have seen him have noted his serious expression.

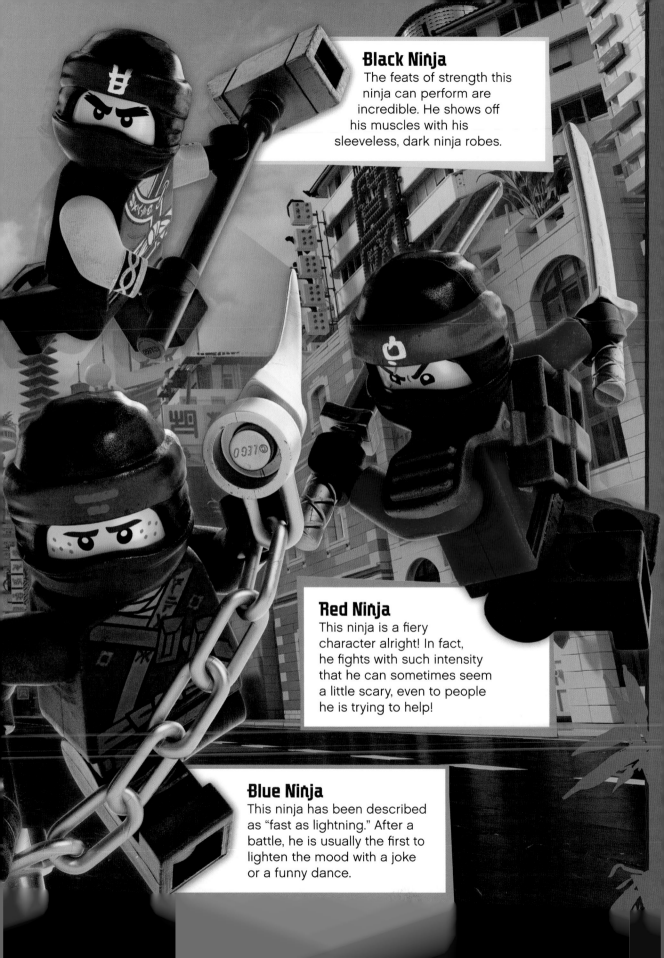

Black Ninja
The feats of strength this ninja can perform are incredible. He shows off his muscles with his sleeveless, dark ninja robes.

Red Ninja
This ninja is a fiery character alright! In fact, he fights with such intensity that he can sometimes seem a little scary, even to people he is trying to help!

Blue Ninja
This ninja has been described as "fast as lightning." After a battle, he is usually the first to lighten the mood with a joke or a funny dance.

LLOYD GARMADON

Secret ninja leader shamed by his name

Life is hard for Lloyd. His villainous dad, Lord Garmadon, left when Lloyd was just a baby. Now, the whole city holds his evil father against him. It is enough to send the average teenager into a sulk. But not Lloyd. He's a ninja and he has a city to save!

All you need is Mom

Lloyd is close to his mom, Koko. She's done a great job of raising him alone. Lloyd wishes he could let her into the secret that he is the Green Ninja. Little does he know that Koko has a secret of her own!

Hood helps block out the sound of his classmates' jokes.

The Green Ninja's signature weapon is a sharp sword.

Lloyd has grown quick on his feet to avoid being noticed.

Lloyd's family tree

Lord Garmadon
Lloyd's absent father is really evil. Maybe it's just as well he stays away.

Koko
Lloyd has a warm, loving mom, but she doesn't like talking about his dad.

Master Wu
His elderly uncle and teacher is sometimes a little too mysterious.

Unpopular with the population

It's not Lloyd's fault his dad is the Worst Guy Ever, but people hold it against him anyway. It's bad enough when his classmates boo him, without his teachers joining in too. No wonder Lloyd likes to hide behind a hood.

Headband bears the Green Ninja's personal symbol.

Green Ninja, ready for Garmadon!

Know the Ninjago language
The characters on the green panel on the edge of Lloyd's robes mean "ninja."

Robust gray armor is worn under ninja robes.

The Green Ninja
Lloyd is the Green Ninja—leader of the Secret Ninja Force. Lloyd isn't sure why Master Wu chose him as leader, but he takes his role very seriously. He wears his green-trimmed robes with pride, and spends hours at sword practice.

LLOYD'S MECH DRAGON

The ninja think technology is the key to beating Lord Garmadon. If they keep making better mechs than his, they will surely win in the end. Master Builder Lloyd builds all their vehicles. None is more awesome than his own mean, green, dragon machine! The Dragon Mech soars through the Ninjago skies, racing to save the day.

Lloyd in control
It takes skill to fly a mech of this size. Lloyd sits at the controls in the cockpit. He operates the dragon's jaws, tail, and weapons while controlling its speed and altitude. With Wu looking on, he doesn't want to make a mistake.

Snapping jaws open and close to grab enemies.

Spiked, swooshing tail is operated by turning a wheel.

All limbs are fully jointed and move independently.

Each foot bears two sharp, golden claws.

Beware the dragon
Most foes are transfixed by the mech's snapping jaws. They rarely notice the missiles on its legs until it's too late. And when the pop-out thrusters fire, the dragon will be on top of them before they know it!

Moving machine
The dragon is made up of jointed segments so it can easily twist, turn, and arch as it flies. Enemy vehicles are no obstacle for this flexible beast.

LLOYD'S HOME

In central Ninjago City, space is hard to come by. Most people live in small apartments in commercial blocks. In Lloyd and Koko's block, the lower floors bustle with shops, banks, cafes, bars, markets, and leisure facilities.

Home... alone

Living at home with Mom does not mean that Lloyd never gets lonely. Everyone apart from his ninja friends rejects him—and that hurts. It's all his dad's fault! Lying in bed at night, Lloyd wishes his dad could be good.

A radio tower with a spire is at the very top of the block.

Lloyd keeps his ninja suit in the roof room of his apartment.

Did you know?

To get from the bottom level to Lloyd's top level, you can take the elevator or phone block, you can take for a flying taxi.

"Stop right there!" A cop in a sushi bar spots a fishy-looking felon.

Hungry Kai enjoys a lovely, fresh-baked croissant.

Lowest level of the block sits alongside narrow canals.

Sushi break

Lloyd and Kai have treated themselves to a sushi break at a local eatery. They're looking forward to an hour of chilling, chatting, and tasty snacks. Let's hope Garmadon doesn't choose this moment to attack!

NYA

The best at being the best

Nya is not just a brilliant fighter and a quick thinker, she's a great motivator too. Rallying the team is one of her finest skills. In fact, it's hard to think of something Nya isn't good at. At least that is what she is quick to tell her brother and fellow ninja, Kai.

Nya vs. Kai arguments

Which is better— fire or water?
Nya knows water can put out Kai's flames in no time!

Who has more fans in the city?
Clearly Silver Ninja fans outnumber Red Ninja fans.

Who is the most humble?
Nya is the best at being humble. She's best at everything.

Always on duty

When Nya isn't being a ninja, she dresses down in casual street clothes. But she is still ready to leap into action if there is trouble in Ninjago City. When a police rickshaw gives chase to a villain, Nya hops aboard to lend a little secret ninja muscle.

Watertight cockpit can rotate around 360 degrees.

Hoverpad-style feet enable the Strider to climb buildings.

Nya's Water Strider

In her bug-like Water Strider, Nya takes any battle in her stride. It walks on water or on land, and can even climb walls. Nya can rotate the cockpit to keep the enemy in sight, then take aim and release a missile from the six-stud rapid shooter. Bullseye!

Long, jointed legs move independently of each other.

Ninja ponytail keeps hair out of Nya's eyes.

I love my job!

Spear has a sharp point at one end and a tassel at the other.

Elbow pads offer protection from cuts and scrapes.

Water warrior

Nya makes sure foes get the point when she goes after them with her mighty spear! Nya's silver Secret Ninja Force armor features an overskirt made of tough, studded fabric to protect her upper legs in battle.

SO NINJA!

After each victory, the ninja celebrate by shouting that they are "so ninja!" They put their success down to their mechs. These high-tech machines are awesome, but they aren't the only thing the ninja need to defeat Garmadon.

Secret store
It is essential to store the mechs away from prying, non-ninja eyes. An old warehouse by Ninjago City docks is the ideal place. The roof opens for access from above.

What makes a mech?
A mech is a robotic machine that is worn or driven. When operated with skill, it almost becomes a part of its owner. Lloyd has built each ninja a custom mech that reflects their personality.

The ice powers of Zane's mech will

Cole maneuvers his mech into tight spots with ease.

Enemies get a shock when caught by a lightning bolt from Jay's mech.

Full force

The mechs are great at defeating enemies. The city's citizens are so grateful to the ninja that they don't mind clearing up the mess left behind. After all, the people of Ninjago City will always rebuild!

When things heat up in battle, Kai's mech is never far away.

Lloyd's Dragon Mech is a welcome sight for

Skillful Nya pilots her Strider through the narrow streets and canals of the city.

POPULAR OPINION

Ninjago City buzzes with songs and stories about the Secret Ninja Force. Their leader, the Green Ninja, is the most popular guy in town. Nobody knows he is really Lloyd Garmadon— the most unpopular guy in town!

These guys are the coolest heroes ever!

That Blue Ninja seems like a nice, polite boy, too!

I want to be just like the Green Ninja!

The ninja make my job a whole lot easier!

Everyone's gone green!
All the ninja have their fans, but the Green Ninja is by far the most popular. He is often the one to deal the final blow that defeats Lord Garmadon. If only he would get rid of Lloyd Garmadon, too!

JAY

He has the skills but he needs to chill

Jay appears chatty and outgoing, but secretly he is filled with doubts. What if his ninja skills aren't up to scratch? When this nervous ninja isn't stressing about that, he's stressing about something else—his admiration for Nya.

> Blue Ninja. Not at all nervous...

Ready in a flash

As the Ninja of Lightning, Jay wears a robe trimmed with electric blue. His orange scarf and leg bindings add striking pops of color. Hours of practice in the dojo have made Jay an expert with his hefty spiked flail.

Knee straps give extra support for high ninja kicks.

Know the Ninjago language

Hidden beneath Jay's cross-body belt are the Ninjago language characters for "spark." Perfect for the Ninja of Lightning!

Jay's Lightning Jet

Bolts of lightning crackle in the sky over Ninjago City. It isn't an electrical storm—it's Jay in his Lightning Jet! This amazing craft has a whirling electro disc to generate energy. Lots of antennae divert the energy at foes. Now that's what you call a bolt from the blue!

Rotating electro disc generates power.

Jay sits in dome-shaped cockpit.

Antennae deliver a shocking blast.

Happy families

Jay is happy that his parents, Ed and Edna, aren't villains like Lloyd's dad is. They are supportive of everything Jay does, even if it is making brave fashion choices like his orange scarf.

Jay's signature weapon is a silver flail.

Jay's biggest worries

Letting his teammates down
He fears making an error that will cost the ninja a victory.

Upsetting Nya
He would be utterly crushed if his crush crushed his hopes.

People finding out about Edna's seashell collection
Not cool, Mom! (They are kind of pretty though...)

BULLETIN BOARD

At Ninjago High School, everyone knows where to go to find out the latest news. The school bulletin board is constantly updated with rules, messages, awards, reminders, and sometimes warnings. Not all of them are placed there by the staff!

FOUND
A green scarf-type thing with a funny symbol on it. Looks a bit like a ninja hood... Collect from the principal's office.

You're the best, Green Ninja!

New menu this week in the school canteen!

Join us for meals inspired by recent events in Ninjago City.

No food fights, please!

* Ninja noodles
* Saucy sharkburgers
* Mecharoni and cheese

What to do in an emergency!

Please remember these procedures in times of city attack.

* Always stick together to stay safe.
* Listen to your teachers at all times.
* Remain in your classroom. Get a hall pass if you and your friends need to leave mysteriously.
* No bullying of anyone at any time. Even if their father is the evil villain destroying the city.

Jay ♥ Nya

DON'T FORGET CAREER DAY NEXT WEEK!

Remember, Friday is **Bring Your Parent to School Day**. We want to hear from your moms and dads about what it's like to be a firefighter, a builder, or a barista in Ninjago City.

P.S. If your last name is Garmadon, DON'T bring your dad to school.

Sponsored by the Master Re-Builders' Association.

TALKS FROM:

Local fisherman gives us the scoop on how he netted his job.

Tea-shop owner pours out wisdom on catering for her thirsty customers.

Ninjago City's biggest rock star chats about life in the music industry.

The Red Ninja rules!

GET LOST GARMABOY!!!

Signed, everyone.

Ninjago High star pupil

Everyone raise a cheer for Zane. He scored 100% in our "Beat the Computer" math challenge. The computer only scored 99.5%.

SCHOOL RULES

NO vehicles on school grounds. Riding motorcycles in the corridors is not allowed.

NO headphones in class. Please enjoy your music at recess. Loud noise disrupts others.

NO running while inside the school. The only exception is when the city is under attack.

NICE SUSHI YOU!

Part-time staff required in your favorite local sushi shop. Delivery drivers, chefs, and cleaners, please apply in store!

ORDER YOUR SCHOOL PHOTO TODAY

VOLCANO LAIR

Lord Garmadon's volcano lair is more than a home—it's an office, a boardroom, and a military headquarters too. From the outside, the cone-shaped volcano looks mysterious as it rises from the sea. Only a few wisps of smoke hint at the hotbed of activity within.

Volcano lair decorative features

Natural lighting
Flickering flames are so flattering to a tyrant's complexion.

Central heating
No fuel bills to pay here... heating's on the house (or in it).

Unpadded seats
A litte discomfort stops soldiers from nodding off during long speeches.

Tea stays hot forever in this lava-fueled tea urn.

Home is where the heat is

Lord Garmadon enjoys a luxury volcanic lifestyle. Each morning starts with a piping hot breakfast in his nice warm bed. Only his custom volcano-print silk pajamas keep him looking and feeling cool.

Flames cast a not-so-gentle glow over the volcano interior.

Shark Army members fidget on the hard, hot seating tiles.

Volcano dress code

Garmadon likes a tidy-looking team. Soldiers wear dress uniforms with sashes for meetings. Nerds wear clean, white lab coats. Casual clothes are meant to be hidden, but many nerds risk unbuttoning their coats to cope with the heat.

Minions take a General away to be fired from the volcano.

Did you know?

Every vessel in Lord Garmadon's Shark Army has its own spot in a huge garage inside the volcano. From there, they can launch directly into the ocean.

GENERAL #1

Fired when no longer required

General #1 is the top-ranking officer in the Shark Army. He enjoys glory, power, and a chance to bask in Lord Garmadon's evil shadow. There's just one snag. If he upsets his boss, he will be fired. From a volcano. Just like every other General #1 before him.

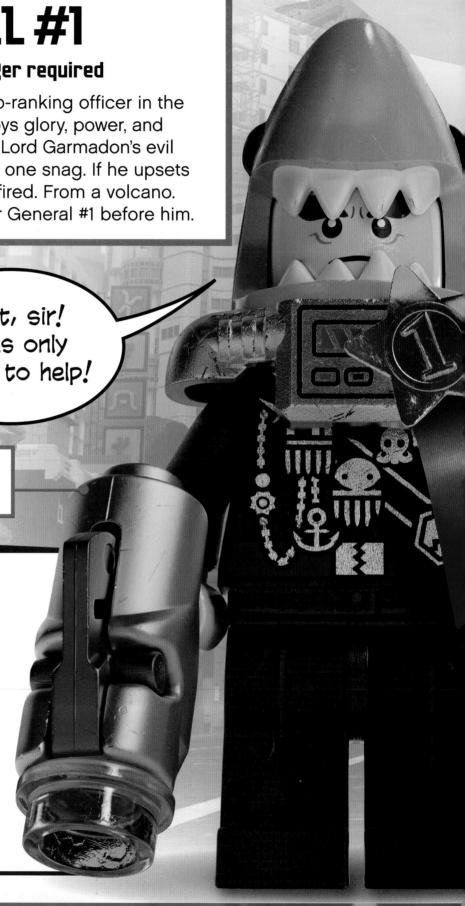

Wait, sir! I was only trying to help!

Large blaster to intimidate lower-ranking soldiers.

Military decorations

It's taken General #1 a long time to climb the ranks, and he's won a lot of medals along the way. He has an anchor medal, a shark medal, and one that looks like a jellyfish. Who knows what grim things he has had to do to earn these rewards?

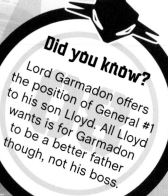

Did you know?

Lord Garmadon offers the position of General #1 to his son Lloyd. All Lloyd wants is for Garmadon to be a better father though, not his boss.

Easy ways to get fired

Let Garmadon's soda go flat
He likes the tongue-tingling taste of the bubbly drink.

Talk about your happy family life
He isn't happy. He has no family. Got it?

Be the perfect employee
Even if you do everything right, the boss might just get bored one day.

Out with the old

Being fired is humiliating. First, two oafs in octopus helmets drag you away. Then you're bundled into position and launched out of the volcano and into the sky. Then... whoa! Where do all these generals land anyway?

Silver shoulder guard is scratched from past battles.

Shiny #1 medal may soon be taken away from the General.

Fruit cocktail has an aftertaste of volcanic lava.

Thin, blue fins surround General #2's head, back, and legs.

In with the new

When a General #1 is fired, the next-in-rank takes their place. This General #2 can't wait for her promotion. She hopes she won't upset Lord Garmadon. Nobody told her he can't stand to see officers slurping drinks on duty.

Fishy scale pattern can be seen under fins.

Cockpit cover

The ninja won't dare approach this mech, but a few extra shields protect the machine just in case.

GARMA MECHA MAN

Lord Garmadon's nerds have designed a mech so huge and so scary that it is sure to have the ninja on the run. It's the Garma Mecha Man! The IT guys are proud of its fearsome features but the boss still has a few suggestions of his own to add. Suggestions? Make that demands.

Hey IT nerds, if I'm going underwater in this, it better be watertight... Lord G (your boss)

IMPORTANT: Must add cup holder for my soda.

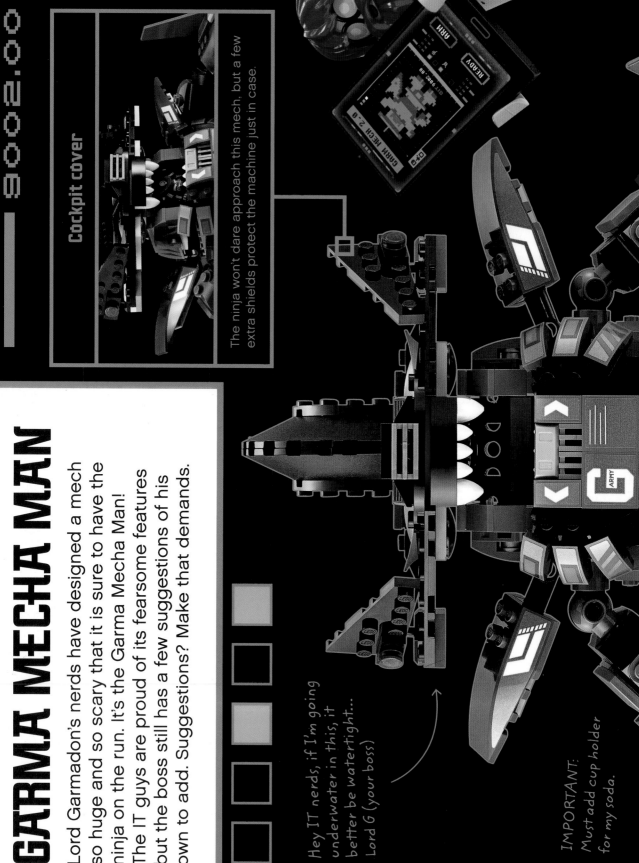

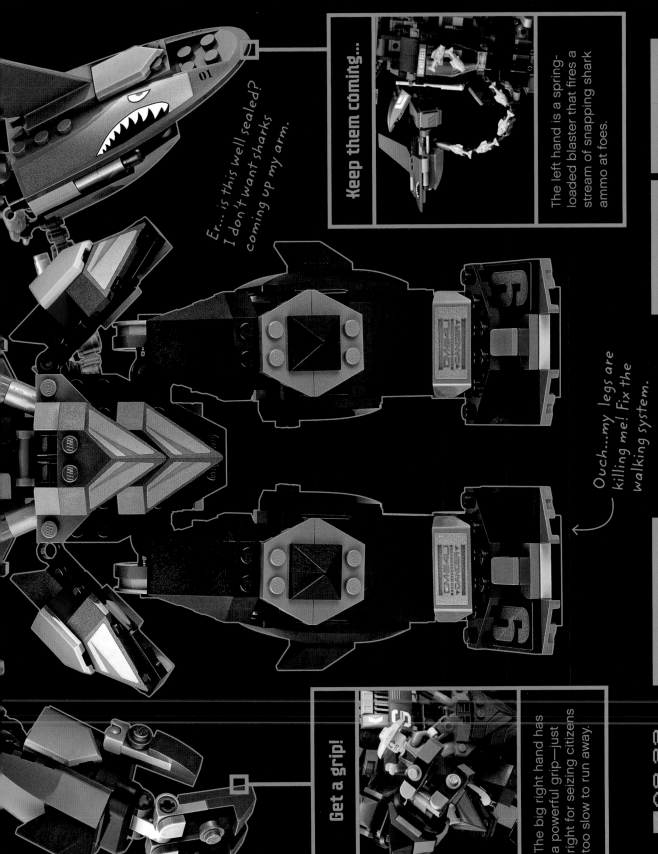

01

Er... is this well sealed? I don't want sharks coming up my arm.

The left hand is a spring-loaded blaster that fires a stream of snapping shark ammo at foes.

Ouch....my legs are killing me! Fix the walking system.

Get a grip!

The big right hand has a powerful grip—just right for seizing citizens too slow to run away.

37

MASTER WU

Training up a new generation of ninja

Wise old Master Wu is training the Secret Ninja Force. It isn't easy. His pupils have not yet grasped that a true ninja relies on what is within, not just on technology. This has given Wu many headaches. Just as well he is an expert in the ninja art of staying calm!

Staff is used for fighting, resting on, and helping with balance.

Weapon rack holds two staffs with tips shaped like hands.

Down in the dojo
Ninja training takes place on Master Wu's boat, *Destiny's Bounty*. The training area is called the dojo. Behind it is a wall with a scroll bearing Master Wu's symbol. Wu put the sign there to help the ninja focus their attention.

Ultimate secret
Master Wu is in possession of the Ultimate Weapon, which could help save Ninjago City from Lord Garmadon. He tries to keep it out of sight of the novice ninja. He worries they do not have the inner skills needed to control it.

Traditional straw hat covers more than a wise old head!

A ninja bends but never breaks.

Wu wear

Modern trends are not for Master Wu. He always wears traditional robes in calming neutral colors. His robe even has a symbol meaning "peace" on the back. Wu's weapon is a low-tech but high-impact wooden staff.

Wu's best ways to stay balanced

Drink tea
Sip your tensions away with a relaxing cup of tea. Ahhhhh...

Play the flute
Soothe yourself with the sweet sound of traditional music.

Meditate
Sit down, close your eyes, breathe deep, and let your mind come to rest.

WARRING WISDOM

The ninja often wish Master Wu's words of wisdom were easier to understand. They are even more confused when Lord Garmadon starts giving them advice, too. The brothers have opposite opinions, but which is the right way for the ninja?

It's what is in your heart that matters.

There is nothing ninja about you ninja.

True ninja don't rely on mechs and missiles.

They practice humility and bravery and tranquility and respect.

Destruction is not the ninja way.

Get yourself
a volcano, kids.

"You kids are going
to need my dark
warlord skills."

"Doing this warlord style
is the only way you're
going to stay alive."

"Warlord pro-tip: Never
give your enemy the
high ground."

"If someone is picking
on you, fire them out
of a volcano."

DESTINY'S BOUNTY

Master Wu's boat is moored at the docks in Ninjago City. Its name is *Destiny's Bounty*. The quaint old boat is decked out with jaunty lanterns, flags, and houseplants. It does not look like a place where a ninja master would live and teach. But that's exactly what it is!

A dragon design is split over the front and middle sails.

Hidden treasures
Ninja training weapons, such as the Green Ninja's sword, are stored in the dojo. But there are other weapons hidden under the deck, too. They include gold and silver katana swords, sharp sais, and spiky shurikens.

Double figurehead has two carved dragons' faces.

Lessons on the water
A safe haven for all the ninja, *Destiny's Bounty* provides the team with a place to practice, relax, and spend time together. It is even a peaceful fishing spot!

Home sweet boat

When he isn't teaching, Master Wu retires to his living quarters at the back of the boat. Clever storage enables him to fit a lot into this small space. There is room for cooking, washing, meditating, and sleeping.

Did you know?

Destiny's Bounty has two anchors. Both can be wound up and then dropped to stop the boat suddenly if it should start to drift.

Fenders on boat stop the hull bashing against the dock walls.

COLE

He's strong, but not exactly silent

Cole is proud to be the strongest ninja, and hones his body with vigorous daily workouts. He's a ninja of few words, but his cool, calm presence lets the others know he is right beside them in times of trouble. Well, that and the loud music he plays.

Beat to the beat!

The cockpit of Cole's mech has a record deck. When DJ Cole spins a disc, loud rock music pours from the speakers, creating shock waves that can floor enemies. When Cole turns up the bass, he puts foes in their place!

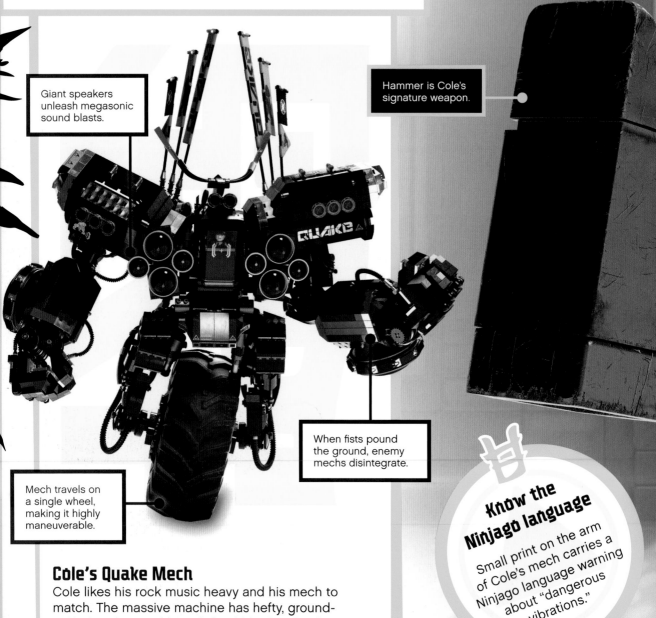

Giant speakers unleash megasonic sound blasts.

Hammer is Cole's signature weapon.

QUAKE

When fists pound the ground, enemy mechs disintegrate.

Mech travels on a single wheel, making it highly maneuverable.

Know the Ninjago language

Small print on the arm of Cole's mech carries a Ninjago language warning about "dangerous vibrations."

Cole's Quake Mech

Cole likes his rock music heavy and his mech to match. The massive machine has hefty, ground-pounding fists and broad shoulders fitted with giant speakers. Even the single wheel is oversized—and it needs to be to support all that weighty tech up top.

We are all so ninja!

Sleeveless top shows off Cole's strong biceps.

Distractions from training

Listening to music
At school, in the dojo, or in battle, Cole usually has his headphones on.

Making music
Cole lays down his own tracks, each perfectly mixed to knock out his foes.

Styling his man-bun
He never forgets to take a selfie to show off when his hair looks so ninja!

Down to earth ninja
This trusty ninja is very grounded, so it is no wonder he is the Ninja of Earth. Cole wears clothes in dark, earthy shades, and fights with a hammer. A lightweight, sleeveless top keeps Cole as cool as he thinks he is.

MY SECRET DIARY

It hurts my feelings when people are mean to me because of who my dad is. I told Master Wu, and he suggested I write everything down in this diary, good and bad. It helps me to remember that although people tease Lloyd, they really, really love the Green Ninja… and that's me, too!

7am Uhhh… not feeling so bright this morning. Another sleepless night wondering what to do about my dad, Garmadon.

7:30 am I wish Mom wouldn't turn the TV on at breakfast. There's usually something bad on about Dad. I've lost my appetite.

DON'T FORGET
- Homework
- Save the city
- Unblock the fire hose on Kai's mech.

8am Here we go… get on the school bus, smile, say hello, find a seat. Ignore it when everyone moves to the other side of the bus.

8:30 am Arrive at school. Wipe off the "Garmadork" graffiti scrawled on my locker and head off to class. At least Cole, Jay, Nya, Kai, and Zane are here.

PROPERTY OF LLOYD GARMADON

2 pm Dad's on the attack... time to save the city again! I feel better now I'm the Green Ninja, I'm in my Dragon Mech, and everyone's cheering me. Wonder how those upgrades are gonna perform?

Take that, Dad!

I SMELL

5 pm Dad called. What could he possibly want to talk about? It turns out he didn't even mean to call me—it was just an accident.

7 pm Yay! Time to chill with my buddies. We talk about today's battle and how awesomely ninja we all are. They don't care who my dad is. I love these guys. I love being a ninja!

SO NINJA!

DO NOT READ!!

CITY BATTLE

Battle is raging in Ninjago City—and it's the worst battle yet! The ninja mechs cannot hold back the dreaded Garma Mecha Man, and it looks as though the city will fall to Lord Garmadon at last. Could things possibly get any worse?

Scarier than sharks!

The Shark Army streams through the streets, leaving a trail of destruction. They are about to learn that something even more destructive is coming. A beast is in the city—and the city might not be a very safe place for a fish!

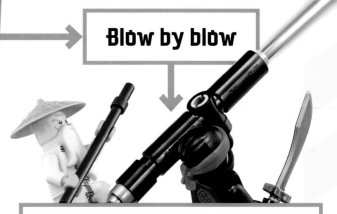

Disobeying orders
Lloyd is desperate not to let his dad win this battle. He disobeys Master Wu and tries to use the Ultimate Weapon on Garmadon. It doesn't work quite how Lloyd expects!

I wish you weren't my father!
Lord Garmadon gloats over Lloyd's failure, prompting Lloyd to angrily reveal his true identity. He utters the devastating words "I wish you weren't my father!"

Beast on the loose
While Garmadon reels at Lloyd's words, a beast summoned by the Ultimate Weapon rampages through the city. Citizens flee as buildings crash down all around them.

KAI

Hothead who's hot on the battlefield

Kai is always rushing into things and taking crazy risks. He says he's bold—others say he's reckless! He must learn that when he puts himself in danger, he puts the team in danger too. He might even be putting that well-styled hair of his in danger. Whoah!

The heat is off

When the battle is over (and hopefully won), it's time to chill. Kai and his teammates head back to the Mech Garage to relax and unwind. Kai's mech-sized recliner chair is a welcome sight for a worn-out ninja.

Icon on flag contains the Ninjago language symbols for "Kai."

Fire blasters shoot flames from the mech's hands.

Kai's favorite conversation topics

The Red Ninja
Kai loves to recount stories of his daring moves in battle.

Red Ninja fans
Kai is always looking out for Red Ninja fans in crowds of cheering citizens.

What's for dinner?
Croissants, sushi, or tacos, Kai loves trying new dishes.

Monumental mech

Glossy, red, and terrifyingly tall, Kai's Fire Mech can scorch a path through enemy lines in no time. Disc shooters on its shoulders take out far-off foes, while fire blasters on the arms melt enemy mechs that dare to get too close.

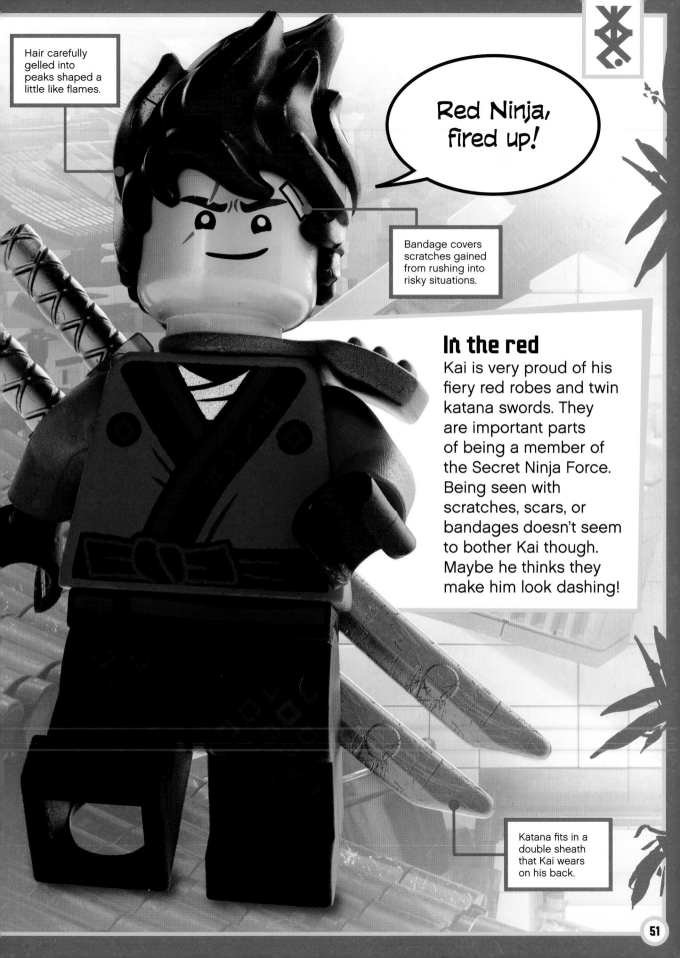

PERILOUS JOURNEY

What is more powerful than the Ultimate Weapon? The Ultimate Ultimate Weapon, of course! It could save Ninjago City, but to find it the ninja must make a long and perilous journey across Ninjago Island. Master Wu is not sure they have what it takes, but the ninja want to try. Onward, ninja!

Volcano Lair

Avoid!

You must leave the safety of the city...

enter dense jungles teeming with unnamed horrors...

Ninjago City

Ninja, turn back! Don't end up like me!

Jungle

and climb to the top of a shaky, quaky temple!

Temple guard dogs

Temple of the Ultimate Ultimate Weapon

Pass over tall, cloud-shrouded mountains...

Master Falls

cross turbulent waters and battle weird, wild foes...

THE JUNGLE

Welcome to the jungle—the deep, dense, Ninjago jungle. The ninja are here in search of the Ultimate Ultimate Weapon that could help save their city. But in this weird, wild place and with no mechs to rely on, they're way out of their comfort zone.

Farewell, Ninjago City

The ninja have no choice but to enter the scary jungle to fulfill their mission. Before they do, they turn and wave goodbye to their beloved city. They wave goodbye to their mechs, gadgets, and technology too. Oh no!

Did you know?
The Ninjago jungle is known by some as the "Forest of Whispers." Master Wu has excellent hearing but the ninja must learn how to listen to the natural world.

There's quite a drop at this end of the bridge. Watch out!

Danger everywhere!

There's lots to watch out for in the jungle. Wild animals. Poisonous plants. Bandits. Rickety bridges. Maybe even Lord Garmadon, desperate to get his hands on the Ultimate Ultimate Weapon before the ninja can.

A bamboo cage is a useful tool if you need to catch a villain.

Jungle master

Master Wu is quite at home in the jungle. In tune with nature, he can sense danger as it approaches. Wu knows that the ninja must master this skill too, but it is a lesson they must learn on their own.

A hidden skeleton holds a secret map. That could be useful!

A fall onto these pointy rocks could dent more than your pride.

ZANE

Robot ninja who's always chilled

Who is the coolest ninja of all? That's Zane, the Ninja of Ice. This archer is a robot, a video player, and a walking calculator. He's a good pal too, offering "friendly companionship mode" to his teammates in good times or bad.

Know the Ninjago language

The Ice Mech features a clue to its owner's identity. A sign near the cockpit features symbols meaning "Zane."

Only human

Zane would love to experience life as a normal teen. His robot sensors help him to mimic human behavior, but sometimes misfire. It's awkward when you realize you laughed at something that wasn't a joke.

Cool guy; hot shot! Zane's bow fires freezing arrows at foes.

Ice Tank

Zane scores many crushing victories in his Ice Tank, thanks to its giant, mech-mashing tracks. A rotating container at the back provides its rapid shooter with a steady supply of icy ammo to freeze foes as they flee.

Ice cannon has a six-stud rapid shooter.

Tracks crush enemy mechs like a mallet crushes ice.

White, flat-top hairstyle conceals robot circuitry.

I am programmed to kick butt!

White-clad warrior

Laundry detergent must top Zane's shopping list. His white costume is simply spotless! Zane's weapon is a bow and arrow. With the robot ability to control speed and trajectory, this awesome archer always hits his mark.

Zane's special robot skills

Recognizing emotions
Programming enables him to tell smiles from snarls.

Keeping quiet
Zane switches on "silent mode" when Master Wu asks for quiet in the dojo.

Instant calculations
Can be offputting when he calculates ninja chances of success as "zero."

TEMPLE

Deep in the jungle stands the ancient Temple of the Ultimate Weapon. It contains a glorious prize, but it also contains many hazards. Will the ninja find what they are looking for inside its walls? If they do, will they make it out again?

Ancient Ninjago features such as roof carvings are rare in the city.

Temple traps

Finding the jungle temple is tricky enough. Getting to the top is even trickier. The ninja must dodge a trap door, rock dropper, dynamite dropper, blade shooters, sword trap, and hanging cage along the way.

Guard dogs

Two fearsome stone dogs guard the temple. These horrible hounds are trained to scare off intruders. Few people are brave enough to discover that they can be easily tamed with a tickle on the tummy!

Did you know?

Master Wu warned his students about the Temple of Fragile Foundations. The ninja better watch their step as they explore.

The library contains an old, mysterious scroll.

Lloyd searches everywhere for the Ultimate Ultimate Weapon.

Wall art gives clues about the temple's former residents.

LESSONS FROM THE JUNGLE

For city kids like the ninja, the jungle is a strange and unfamiliar place. They will have to learn some lessons quickly—and that's just to survive, let alone to fulfill their mission. Come to think of it, the jungle holds a few important lessons for those who have been here before, too.

We are one with the elements.

Nya
I've learned to be less competitive. Getting through the jungle together safely was all that mattered. Wu's lessons were key to keeping us all safe.

Kai
I've learned to keep quiet—sometimes for even more than thirty seconds! You never know when a listening enemy is hiding in the undergrowth, so stealth is vital.

We're ready!

Cole
The sounds of the jungle can tell you a lot about who and what is around you. I've learned to take my headphones off and replace them with a cunning disguise.

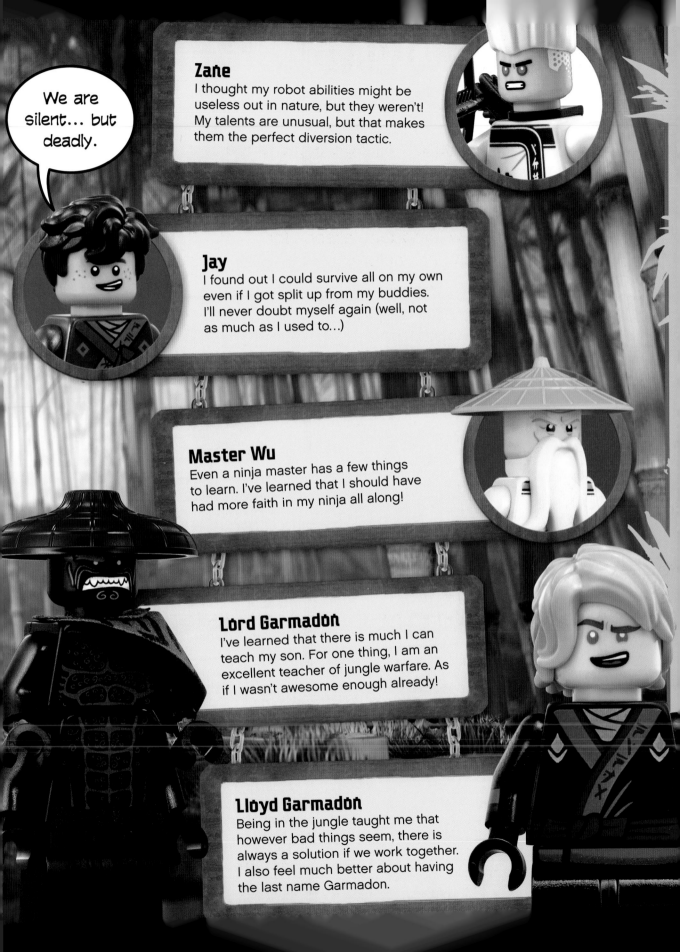

We are silent... but deadly.

Zane
I thought my robot abilities might be useless out in nature, but they weren't! My talents are unusual, but that makes them the perfect diversion tactic.

Jay
I found out I could survive all on my own even if I got split up from my buddies. I'll never doubt myself again (well, not as much as I used to...)

Master Wu
Even a ninja master has a few things to learn. I've learned that I should have had more faith in my ninja all along!

Lord Garmadon
I've learned that there is much I can teach my son. For one thing, I am an excellent teacher of jungle warfare. As if I wasn't awesome enough already!

Lloyd Garmadon
Being in the jungle taught me that however bad things seem, there is always a solution if we work together. I also feel much better about having the last name Garmadon.

ACKNOWLEDGMENTS

Editor Beth Davies
Designer Sam Bartlett
Pre-Production Producers Siu Yin Chan
and Jennifer Murray
Producer Louise Daly
Managing Editor Paula Regan
Design Manager Jo Connor
Art Director Lisa Lanzarini
Publisher Julie Ferris
Publishing Director Simon Beecroft

DK would like to thank Randi Sørensen, Paul Hansford,
Martin Leighton Lindhardt, Heidi K. Jensen, and Simon Lucas at
the LEGO Group; Ben Harper at Warner Bros.; and Emma Grange
and Jenny Edwards at DK for editorial and design assistance.

First American Edition, 2017
Published in the United States by DK Publishing
345 Hudson Street, New York, New York 10014

A catalog record for this book is available from
the Library of Congress.

ISBN: 978-1-4654-6117-9

DK books are available at special discounts when purchased in
bulk for sales promotions, premiums, fund-raising, or educational
use. For details, contact: DK Publishing Special Markets,
345 Hudson Street, New York, New York 10014
SpecialSales@dk.com

Printed and bound in the USA

A WORLD OF IDEAS:
SEE ALL THERE IS TO KNOW

www.LEGO.com
www.dk.com